Four Brown Bear Cubs: Mother
Bear Sharing Salmon With Cubs

Four Brown Bear Cubs: Mother Bear Sharing Salmon With Cubs

. . .

Bob Benda

ISBN: 1499164262
ISBN 13: 9781499164268

I live in Valdez, Alaska. I have watched and photographed this female coastal brown bear and her four cubs for three years. During their first year the mother catches salmon to share with the cubs. The cubs start catching their own salmon during their second year. This photo shows the female brown bear and her four cubs at the Solomon Gulch Hatchery. Mom and the cubs frequently visited the hatchery during the summer to feed on returning pink salmon. Hatchery reared salmon return to the hatchery after feeding in the ocean. They swim into the hatchery. There they are spawned, incubated, hatched, reared, and released into the ocean in spring. After release they spend time in the ocean before returning to the hatchery.

The cubs are about 6 months old. They learn how to catch salmon by watching their mother catch them. She feeds the cubs and herself. This photo shows her entering the water in search of fish.

She is almost totally underwater trying to catch a pink salmon.

Mom is all wet, but she was successful. She caught a pink salmon for her and the cubs to eat.

Water drips from her fur as she starts to bring the pink salmon to shore.

She's onshore. You can see how much water is dripping off her fur. The cubs are watching her. They start walking toward her to share the catch. They know it's time to eat.

She carried the salmon farther onshore. She is still dripping water from her dive. The cubs are running after her to get their share of the salmon.

Mom tore the salmon into pieces for the cubs to eat. You can see how long her claws are in this photo.

Mom picked up the fish and started to walk away from the cubs. The cubs looked for pieces of the salmon in the rocks. The cubs and mom all shared the catch.

She decided to turn around and take the remains of the salmon to eat herself. She let the cubs finish eating the pieces of salmon in the rocks.

The salmon is in pieces. Mom has the tail in her mouth. If you look carefully between the legs of the cub walking away, you can see it's carrying a large piece of the salmon. The other three cubs are picking pieces from between the rocks.

The cub walked away with the piece of salmon. It left mom and the other three cubs. One of the remaining cubs is trying to take the mother bear's piece of salmon.

While the cub watches her she eats the rest of her piece of salmon. Now the salmon is all gone and mom will have to try and catch another one.

While mom walks away the cubs finish eating the pieces of salmon in the rocks.

The mother bear went back into the water to try and catch another salmon. You can see the backs of the pink salmon in the water.

Mom didn't have to dive into the water like the last time. It's shallower here. She just had to put her head underwater trying to catch a salmon.

Success! She caught another pink salmon. Only her head and legs got wet this time instead of her whole body.

She turned around in the water and headed back to shore. Will she share the salmon with the cubs or eat it heself?

She's wet again and shedding the water from her fur.

Rather than take the salmon to the cubs she starts to eat the salmon when she gets onshore. I guess she's hungry and wants her share first before the cubs get there.

While she's eating the salmon, one of the cubs comes up to get its share of the fish.

Another cub joined the mother bear and the cub. Each cub grabbed a piece of salmon mom hadn't eaten. Mom just looks away like she wonders what is going on.

After looking away mom decides she wants more of the salmon she caught. Will the other two cubs join them?

The smallest cub didn't join mom and the other two cubs. It found its own piece of salmon. I have observed that this cub is very independent. Many times I watched it go off on its own rather than stay with mom and the other three cubs.

Mom and the other three cubs finished eating the salmon she caught. They walked back along the shore to where the smallest cub was eating the piece of salmon it found.

Mom and the three cubs started walking back along the hatchery raceway wall. The smallest cub picked up its piece of salmon and walked the other way.

As the littlest cub walks away mom and the other cubs follow it. Mom seems like she wants some of the smallest cub's fish.

The smallest cub keeps walking away. It doesn't seem to want to share its piece of salmon with mom or the other cubs.

The smallest cub took its piece of salmon and walked over to the large rock by the water.

The smallest cub started eating its piece of salmon. One of the other cubs looks like it wants to share it.

The smallest cub doesn't want to share its salmon and walks away from the other cub.

Another cub arrived to join the two other cubs. One of the cubs started reaching in trying to grab a piece of the salmon.

The third cub joined the other cubs. They all seem to want to share the smallest cub's piece of salmon. It didn't want to share it. It stopped and continued eating it.

The smallest cub picked up its piece of salmon and walked away from the other three cubs. Two of the cubs are licking up little pieces of salmon off the rock. The third cub continued walking after the smallest cub.

While the three cubs tried to get some of the smallest cub's salmon, mom caught another pink salmon.

Mom climbed up on the rock and shook the water off her fur. One of the cubs gave up following the smallest cub and joined mom on the rock.

Mom and the one cub walk off the rock. She is carrying the salmon farther up on the shore.

Mom starts to eat the pink salmon. The cub that was following her looks like it may help her eat it.

Mom and two of the cubs eat the salmon she caught. One of the other cubs watches the smallest cub eat its piece of salmon. It never did share it with mom or the other cubs.

While mom eats the salmon, all four cubs join her to finish eating it. This ended their feeding for the day and they left the area.

ALASKA COASTAL BROWN BEAR FACTS

1. Alaska coastal bears are called "brown bears".
2. Alaska inland and lower 48 States brown bears are called "grizzly bears".
3. The largest Alaska coastal brown bears are in the Kodiak archipelago islands.
4. A male brown bear is called a boar.
5. A female brown bear is called a sow
6. Brown bears standing on their hind legs are 6-7 feet. Kodiak bears can be over 10 feet.
7. Male brown bears are larger than females (sexual dimorphism).
8. Adult males weigh 300-850 pounds while adult females weigh 200-450 pounds.
9. Kodiak bears can weigh over 1,000 pounds.
10. Brown bears are omnivorous eating grass, berries, mosses, small animals and fish.
11. They prepare for their winter sleep by eating up to 90 pounds of food a day during summer.
12. They gain up to 3 pounds/day of body fat to prepare for sleeping during the winter.
13. Bears will wake up during the winter. They do not enter true hibernation, but deep sleep.
14. Brown bears live 20 to 25 years in the wild.

15. Brown bears mature at 5 years. Males and females are solitary except during mating.
16. The female gives birth in the den during the winter sleep.
17. Typically they give birth to two cubs, but can have up to four cubs. The cubs stay with the mother for 2 to 4 years, depending on when she mates again.
18. Female brown bears have been observed adopting orphaned cubs. This rarely happens, but has been observed twice in Alaska. Once at Katmai National Park and Preserve in September 2014 and years ago on Kodiak Island. Alaska Dispatch News September 16, 2014 "Supermom' grizzly adopts yearling www.ADN.com .
19. The cubs have to avoid the male during mating and may leave the mother at that time.
20. Additional facts can be found at http:/www. pbs.org/wnet/nature/episodes/bears

www.ingramcontent.com/pod-product-compliance
Lightning Source LLC
Chambersburg PA
CBHW051129290526
45796CB00004B/17